I0784916

BERRIES FROM BRAMBLES

BERRIES FROM BRAMBLES

Collection #12

ADDISON STREET WRITERS CIRCLE

Addison Street Writers Circle Publications

Copyright @ 2022 by the Addison Street Writers Circle

All Rights Reserved. No part of this book may be reproduced in any manner whatsoever without written permission except in the case of brief quotations embodied in critical articles and reviews.

For additional information about the Addison Street Writers Circle, including permission to reproduce selections from this booklet, please contact Vivian Pisano: vpisano@lmi.net

ISBN 970-8-9850130-0-9

Contents

PREFACE

Hello,

Who sent out the link?

I can see you but not hear you.

Look for the camera icon on the bottom... Can you press that?

Please mute yourselves, unless you are talking.

Kate, you're on mute!

We can't hear you.

We can't see you.

Is Maryly coming today?

Who's turn is it to send the link?

Anna, are you there? We can see your room, but not you.

Maybe just one of us should send the link?

Has anyone heard from Ruth?

Who will call Martina?

Is it too late to buy stock in Zoom?

The ASWC has remained a strong, committed group of ten writers, apart, but together on Zoom. As writing groups go, we are formidable, now in our twelfth year.

As true Californians, we discuss not only our writing, but vaccination strategies and escape routes in case of fire. We are all vaccinated and have GO bags at the ready. We were relieved by last November's election. The East Bay's cooler temperatures this summer have kept us all a little safer and breathing freely. And yet, despite the national waves of red and blue such as insurrection in the Capitol, vaccination non-believers, devastating wildfires, the costly and wasteful recall election, the worldwide struggles with a pandemic and a number of personal challenges, we have remained steady in our practice. We meet on Zoom, still. No matter the responsibilities or issues that may take us away for a week or three or six, we always return. Tap that keyboard! Indeed, two of our members will be publishing books: Karen this fall, and Vivian, in the new year.

We are mindful of what we lose on Zoom as well. Impromptu chats, lunches together, real eye contact, personal style, and home context are all a part of the camaraderie that we no longer enjoy.

In this, our twelfth year of *Berries from Brambles*, we are transitioning from our DIY format to a self-published book. The ASWC is starting its second decade with its own publishing venture: Addison Street Writers Circle Publications. No longer are we printing copies only for our ourselves, our friends and family; this year's *Berries from Brambles* is available for purchase from Amazon's and

Ingram's distribution channels. If successful, subsequent years' Berries will be similarly published. We owe our heartfelt thanks to Vivian Pisano, who is leading us in this new endeavor.

Last year, thanks to Maryly Snow, we were honored to have UC Berkeley's Bancroft Library agree to carry our past and forthcoming issues of *Berries from Brambles*. The title *Berries from Brambles* and the author, Addison Street Writers Circle, have been catalogued, but it's still in technical processing. We are hopeful to see the addition of our individual names as authors, as well as a classification/call number. Once catalogued, the issues will undoubtedly be available only on site at the Bancroft Library.

In spite of the pandemic and personal issues, here are our writing-related highlights of 2021:

Sue Ezekiel continues to write memoir pieces about her life experience for her self-understanding and for her family and friends' enjoyment. A recent road trip with her husband through numerous national parks was the highlight of her year and, possibly, her next writing project.

Karen Grassle was diagnosed with breast cancer in the winter of 2020, in the midst of preparing her memoir, *Bright Lights, Prairie Dust,* for publication. She published her essay "Grateful for a Mammogram" at nextavenue.org in May 2021. This year has provided her an education in what goes into the actual making of a book before it sees the bookstores. Time-consuming tasks have flooded her inbox, and her writing, ironically, has suffered. While exciting, it's not really what she had in mind. She was thrilled to welcome her ASWC colleagues and friends from the community at the Book Passage launch and reading on November 14.

Ruth A. Hanham, who has been on leave for half of the year, is delighted to return to the ASWC fold. Lately, she's been writing some short autobiographical pieces, some for family consumption only.

Eleanor Lew has used her professional training and writing skill to examine the hate and racism rife in our culture. While she considers possible ways to change immutable human nature, she has also chosen to select pieces from earlier years in ASWC to polish and edit.

Vivian Pisano completed her manuscript, *Living in Two Worlds: A Memoir*. Her self-published book will appear early next year. Vivian has created a website to share news and further writings. Her story, "A Sunday Dinner Outing," was longlisted for the Fish Short Memoir Prize.

Kate Pope writes occasional new memoir pieces and polishes work written earlier in her ASWC years; describing her many travels and mountain adventures. This Spring, two local magazines, *Berkeley Hills Living* (February 2021) and *Berkeleyside* (May 2021) published her work, "Jab at the Bulb," a celebration of her second COVID vaccine shot at the Albany Bulb.

Anna Rabkin was encouraged to write a comparison piece about her late husband, Marty, and his father, Bill Rabkin, who was profiled in a 1948 edition of *The New Yorker*. Her exploration of the lives and times of these two highly individualistic, innovative and much-admired men resulted in a 7000-word essay which she has shared with family and friends. Anna is also collaborating with her brother, Arthur Rose, on the history of their paternal family. Although their father and his nine siblings all perished in the Holocaust, fortuitously two thirds of their children survived. Some stayed in Europe, and others emigrated to Israel, Canada, South America and the United States, where they created surprisingly diverse lives. In January 2020, Anna started and continues a monthly Zoom interview for FAB members whose books have been published, and she is writing profiles of FAB members for the FAB Newsletter.

Martina Reaves' year was unfortunately truncated by a stroke on May 1, 2021. Language was her main loss. Haikus became her forte, indeed "Haiku Stroke" tells of her experience. She has been working diligently with her speech therapist and has made significant strides. We look forward to welcoming her back, full strength, in January.

Maryly Snow says that the Pandemic lockdown was the perfect time to write. But that's not what she did. She spent the first fifteen months focused on her Zentangles group with weekly lessons, while she continued drawing her *Pandemic Paradox series*, created an online store (www.snowstudios.com/store.html), churned out greeting cards, pot holders, and tended to her bees. But did she write? Barely. Rarely. What little she did write disappeared along with her laptop and jewelry in an early 2021 house robbery. She especially laments the disappearance of her "Covid's Rabbit Hole" piece (the continuation of her 2020 *Berries* submission) This paucity leads her toward a semi-concerted, renewed effort towards writing about her art life. But first she has to "Finagle a Fence."

Linda Northrup Sondheimer has been hauling herself around, one-footed, on all the vehicles and safety measures she installed for her husband; walker, wheelchair, etc. Two surgeries for the arthritis in her feet, have resulted in three months in a cast on her left foot and, subsequently, the same for her right foot. Her submission "Is it Time?" is an attempt to put some lightheartedness into the day. She has put aside her fiction and has been working on a memoir, chronicling the last year of her husband's life, and death. It was an arduous but enviable year, their last loving chapter together.

We hope you enjoy the readings herein.

LINDA SONDHEIMER

Anna Rabkin. A Gift from the Past.
> *Secret writing during Nazi occupation of Paris.*

Ruth Hanham. Miseries and Mysteries.
> *Coming of age in the 1950s.*

Kate "Cricket" Pope. The Summit Is in the Doing.
> *A quixotic attempt on Mt. Whitney's East Face.*

Vivian Pisano. Smitten at Thirteen.
> *A young girl's first love experience shapes the woman she becomes.*

Linda Sondheimer. Is It Time?
> *A few self-deprecating laughs in a tough year.*

Eleanor Lew. Black-Tie Gala: What I Think of You And What I Think You Think of Me.
> *Pleasing and appeasing at a soirée.*

Maryly Snow. Finagling a Fence.
> *Trying to negotiate property issues.*

Karen Grassle. A Tree in the Dark.
> *A woman with breast cancer lives in the present.*

Sue Ezekiel. My Canine Adventures.
> *A learning curve well-rewarded.*

Martina Reaves. Haiku Stroke.
> *Haiku as a recovery from a stroke.*

A GIFT FROM THE PAST

The gift of a "locked" faux red leather diary thrilled me. I loved the idea of writing in such a pristine little book. Perhaps, like Anne Frank, I thought of it as the best friend that I lacked. In 1950 it became the safe depository of my boarding school teenage angst, the non-judgmental recipient of my questioning mind and my heart's confusion. I had touching trust that the toy-sized key kept my writing safe from snooping, intolerant eyes. Re-reading those irregular jottings as an older teenager brought into vivid focus forgotten concerns, misunderstandings and thrills. Sadly, my juvenile diary was lost during my peripatetic life.

Fortunately, my relative, Raymonde Rose's diary, daringly kept during the Occupation of Paris, was not lost. Her grandson, David, a university student, found it in 1998 hidden under linens in a wardrobe. He read it and recognized its historic value. Eighty years after his grandmother started it, her diary has been published.

I knew Raymonde and her husband, my cousin Simon, because I spent happy, lazy, and educational summers from 1948 to 1952 at a former farmhouse they had turned into a vacation retreat near the city of Auxerre. On my first visit I was thirteen and their daughter, Dany was three. I thought of her as my little sister.

Raymonde's father, Pepe, produced fresh vegetables from the garden and her mother, Meme, mouth-watering meals from the kitchen. For me, orphaned at an early age, those summers were my first experience of living in an extended loving, argumentative and sometimes mysteriously tight-lipped family. Raymonde and her parents had an obviously close, caring relationship; their relationship with Simon was not without conflict. He worshipped his wife in his own macho way, but she, an artist, a sensitive soul with unexplained ailments constantly carped about his "vulgar speech," his lack of tact, his dirty nails!

Eventually, I moved to New York. On a trip to Paris in 1977 I saw Raymonde and her daughter, Dany for the last time. It was the only time I met Dany's three-year-old son David. My visit with Dany was troubling. She accused me of having been negligent when I took her, a seven-year-old, to a swimming pool in Paris. She had slipped on the metal stairs and gashed her forehead. Twenty-five years later, she turned toward me, and pointed to her face, "See, I have been scarred for life and have had to cope with this ugliness daily." I was shocked and disturbed. Having looked closely at her forehead I saw no scar. I felt she was losing touch with reality.

Raymonde and Dany stopped communicating with extended family. The only news came through a cousin who penetrated the wall of silence. I learned that Raymonde had become an invalid and increasingly reclusive and that Simon looked after her devotedly. Then news of Dany's mysterious illness reached me; she had to live in a nursing home and eventually in a dementia unit.

Raymonde died in 1997 at the age of eighty-seven. Simon aged ninety-two followed a year later. I was losing the people I loved who had filled my teenage summers with happiness.

After my early abortive attempts at keeping a diary, I have relied on my calendars and datebooks to keep track of my activities. Although I have clear memories of my childhood, those datebooks and my collection of photos were invaluable in jogging my memory of my adult years when I started to write my memoir of my survival of the Holocaust in Poland, my improbable trajectory through English boarding schools, spending summers in France, to exploring the world as a New York travel agent and eventually settling in Berkeley and being elected to public office. My book, *From Kraków to Berkeley; Coming out of Hiding,* was published in 2018 in London.

Then out of the blue, in 2020, early in the Covid pandemic I received an email from Dany's son, David, "Thank you so much for writing your precious and interesting book. As you noted in your memoir, my mother started to have serious psychological problems in the early 1980s. She is psychotic and depressed. She's been better since she was in a retirement home."

In a follow up email, he told me that in 1998 he stumbled upon Raymonde's diary while helping to empty his grandparents' apartment. David gave the two notebooks to his mother who evinced little interest in them. But David took them to the Shoah Museum in Paris. The staff was excited. No Jewish diaries written during the Occupation in Paris had been found. David as a lawyer and historian was encouraged to write an analytical introduction and have the diary published.

Over the ensuing years David, set out to do academic research to put Raymonde's diary entries into a historic context and used his knowledge of the family to interpret some of the personal stories. In a subsequent email I received a surprise gift from the past. He attached a PDF of Raymonde's diary and wrote that he was looking for a publisher.

I was both curious and reticent about reading it remembering my locked diary and how I protected it from prying eyes. But curiosity won out. Raymonde started to write her diary shortly after her marriage to Simon in May 1939. Not only did she write about her feelings as a newly married woman in her late twenties adapting to living with a man who was not of the same "sensitivity" as she, but she also had to face the reality of September 3, 1939. France had declared war against Germany. Simon, who was born in Poland, was drafted that October to train with the Polish unit of the French army. He left for the front March 1940. On June 14, 1940 the Germans occupied Paris and on the 22nd the armistice agreement was signed.

Immediately, Simon became a POW. Raymonde anxiously awaited letters. Only in August 1940 did she learn his whereabouts. Throughout the war and his imprisonment, the diary tracks her commitment; she treasured each letter, postcard, or scrap of news about him. She went to great length to save her and her parents' meager rations and to find black market food to send to him as he was moved from one German labor camp to another.

The pages of the diary include clippings from various Paris newspapers, warnings to university students who dared to protest against the Nazi occupation, posters announcing round-ups of Jews and Bolsheviks, announcements by the Vichy regime restricting Jewish life to prisonlike conditions, antisemitic letters to the editor, an article announcing Franklin and Eleanor Roosevelt's Jewish antecedents, and one about the razor slashing of a Jewish painting. Maps showing where the Allies were attacking the Axis forces indicated that Raymonde followed the war closely.

She writes about her joy at being encouraged in 1941 to submit her work for a museum show. When she arrived with her drawings she was asked for "her signature and a declaration that she is not Jewish." She writes that she felt faint, but recovered and said with lying smile, "since I am Jewish, I cannot sign." She felt betrayed and enveloped in tormenting sadness.

Her remarks about her frail physical and emotional health make keeping the diary doubly brave. Her ironic comments about current events, her literary references, her love for her parents and her gratitude for the care Simon's uncle and aunt had shown her, are threads that create a rich portrait of an intelligent, educated and sensitive woman trying to cope during the dangerous, dehumanizing hell that she had to navigate.

Shortly after the victory of the Russians over the Germans in Stalingrad, Raymonde wrote no more. February 14, 1943 is the last entry, "Luckily we are having an ideal winter, because our ration of coal is less than lavish."

We now know that the humiliating loss in Russia led to vengeful retaliation against the Jews. Had her situation in Paris become even more precarious? Did she stop writing because of ill health, fear, despair? How did she survive the Nazis escalating deportations? How did she and her parents live in Paris until Liberation on August 24, 1944? So many unanswered questions. We will never know because Raymonde refused to talk about the war years.

In June 2021 David sent me the published book, *Journal d'une Juive Française à Paris sous l'Occupation*, and it brought back memories of my research in 2003 in Parisian archives and libraries. I was working on my thesis *A Woman of Foreign Affairs*, about the life of the well-known biographer and journalist, Antonina Vallentin. She survived the war in hiding in Vichy France, but left no record of her travails. Doing that research raised my appreciation for primary sources like diaries, journals, letters, business ledgers, military reports, government records all of which provided contemporaneous information that I used to flesh out her life.

Nowadays, blogs, websites, posts on social media, all are potential links to past generations for family and friends, as well as possible sources for background material for future researchers. Likewise, Raymonde's diary provides valuable testimony for both her family and historians. It enters a well-established canon. Like hers, diaries from early on have been reflective and introspective as well as chronicling events. Samuel Pepys' 17th century diary gives us valuable information about the Great Fire and the Great Plague in London. Perhaps current Covid diaries will be equally important.

Our unreliable memories make diaries vital. They capture experiences, events, feelings as they happen. They allow us to revisit a lived past in vivid detail and some provide significant historic background. Raymonde's diary is all of that, it is a courageous gift from a turbulent past.

ANNA RABKIN

MISERIES AND MYSTERIES

The school janitor had lined up just the right number of folding chairs for us sixth graders along the walls of Cragmont's auditorium: fifteen for the boys, fifteen for the girls. Two high-adrenalin moms kept a watchful eye on things. Our dance teacher, Dart Tinkham, presided — a big-bosomed, middle-aged woman whose high heels made her tilt slightly forward as she demonstrated the steps of the waltz, two-step, foxtrot, and all the other dances thought fundamental to civilization in the 1950s. She had a spirited way of intoning, "Slow, slow, quick, quick, *slow*." I'd be the last to call her charismatic, but she had such a forceful personality she must have taught the piano to play on its own accord because I've no memory of any accompanist.

The lessons took place every two weeks and started at seven in the evening. Every two months, the ritual escalated. Girls wore party dresses and Mary Janes with white socks. The boys appeared in their best clothes, but what I most remember was their slicked-back hair and martyred expressions.

Now the festivities began. One of the presiding maternal deities would shout, "Boys, choose your partners." This was the horrible moment which I suspect most girls of my generation remember all too well. There'd be a rush of boys toward two gratified girls and scarcely any to the rest. One of the mothers would stand up, making sweeping motions with her hand. "Boys, are you blind? Look at all those beautiful girls eager to dance." The shouted-at would sullenly comply.

The drill was for the boy to bow and say, "May I have this dance?" in the tone of someone asking a large sardine to take a twirl. I remember wanting to snap back, "Don't think *I'm* any more eager to dance with a drip like you." Then there were those invariable mismatches as to height, with him facing my flat-as-a-pancake chest and me gazing over his head, my peripheral vision observing much treading on toes. But the worst thing was not to be asked at all. Then, with other rejects, I'd have to flee to the girls' bathroom to comb my hair for the fourth time.

Such "socials" seemed to involve more and more girls because in a mysterious way, the number of boys on the dance floor kept lessening. Inevitably, one of the mothers would shout to the other, "They've done it again!" The two women would charge out of the side doors into the shadowy playground, half-lit by light streaming from the auditorium's windows. It would illumine clumps of boys crouched behind the bushes. "Come on back, boys, do your duty." Another humiliation. Once one of the mothers propelled a boy called Randy toward the sidelines where I was sitting. "Why not choose this delightful girl?"

But instead of asking me to dance, Randy turned to his pal Chip, "I'll give you a nickel if *you* dance with her."

I stood absolutely still. Had I heard correctly? I had. The two boys were smirking at me. Randy snickered. Chip seemed about to join in when he must have noticed my stricken face. He looked ashamed. "Ah, come on, wise guy. I'll dance with her. Keep your darned nickel." So saying, he gave me a conspiratorial wink and squeezing my hand, pulled me toward the dance floor. But could any wink, let alone a friendly squeeze, comfort a girl priced at a nickel?

Why is it that even decades later, I remember those dance lessons with such loathing? Could it be because they ripped the blindfold off my eyes so that I beheld a new reality? Until then, I'd been too sheltered to realize how much the whims of boys and men could determine my standing. Now I became aware that no matter how lovable my inner self, no matter how irreproachable my outward conduct, in Dart Tinkham's world all that mattered were my looks. Yes, through no fault of my own, I could be humiliated by any boy and left on the sidelines, just because he didn't like my appearance.

Another dismaying discovery at these dances was that every girl, whether she liked it or not, had to compete with every other girl for a partner. At dances like this one, even my best friend, even my beloved sisters, might become my rivals.

Finally, came a third revelation, which I am about to describe in the next section. This discovery was to prove far less humiliating than the first two. Whereas every girl competed with every other on the dance floor, this revelation united rather than divided them. Some would argue its effects were also more far-reaching. Or were they? You decide.

It all started one morning as I sat in my 9 a.m., eighth-grade Civics class at Garfield Junior High School (now King Middle School). Being a year ahead, I was only twelve and still preferred collecting stamps to collecting boyfriends. I happened to be daydreaming about owning the world's rarest postage stamp—a one-of-a-kind beauty from British Guiana, mauve in color and irregular in shape—when a Big Brother voice came over the loudspeaker system, "Attention, all girls in the seventh, eighth, and ninth grades, you are to report to the gym at 10 a.m. for a special meeting."

At the appointed hour, a large assemblage of girls shuffled into the familiar school gym. We eased ourselves down onto its polished wood floor and waited with crossed legs as we chattered away like migrating warblers that have just discovered some well-stocked branches of pyracantha berries.

A hush descended when pudgy Mrs. Myra Hofstadter strode in, her whistle on its lanyard swinging back and forth. She stationed herself in front of us. Her eyes smoldered.

"Girls, I wouldn't have thought it possible. I was under the impression that you came from respectable Berkeley homes. *Respectable* Berkeley homes!"

A low murmur. We didn't like her tone of voice.

"Yes, the school janitor has had a word with me. I don't need to tell you what about. He just doesn't like it, and I sympathize. So, wrap *them* up before you put them in the metal receptacle. Is that clear? It better be."

Indignation welled up in me. I was used to fairness at home. I'd done nothing wrong that I knew of. Why scold me?

We filed out. The other girls were muttering in a grumpy sort of way. Everybody but me seemed to understand what Mrs. Hofstadter had been talking about. I felt too abashed to ask anyone. Wrap what up? That evening, as I rubbed Clearasil into my latest pimple, the best explanations I could come up with seemed feeble. Had she meant we were supposed to wrap our icky banana peels around half-eaten sandwiches before dropping them into the garbage? Ridiculous! Why waste time dumping garbage into yet more garbage? Why force this message on girls but not boys? And what did "respectable homes" have to do with it? In fact, why hire such an over-fastidious janitor in the first place?

Another mystery also made me yearn for the help of that iconic sleuth, Nancy Drew. What, for example, was the meaning of those full-page ads in *The Ladies Home Journal* which every month featured a different beauty, always wearing a magnificent evening dress. The February goddess, posed under a chandelier, might flaunt, say, a cobalt-blue satin dress with elaborate ruffles around the neckline. Her March successor might swan about in a ballgown fashioned from raspberry taffeta. What did it all mean? I wondered. Why that half-smile on their faces? Why their air of knowingness? The only clue consisted of a slogan at the bottom of the page which read, "*Modess because....*" Because what? Talk about mysteries!

I confided my confusion to my best friend, Fran Lindsay. She looked thoughtful and invited me over to her house in about two weeks' time. When we entered its carpeted living room, I was astonished to see her mother sitting on the sofa, as if waiting for us. Usually, we'd find her at the Formica kitchen table, smoking and cutting out food coupons from *Good Housekeeping*. Smiling, she patted the sofa on either side of her. As we sat down, I noticed she looked a little tense. Strange, she was usually so easy-going.

She cleared her throat and said in the husky tones of a chain smoker, "Now, Ruth, for some time Fran and I have gotten the impression that you don't know anything about, well, *what every girl ought to know*. Now, by any chance has your mother had *a very special talk* with you lately?"

I cast around. "Well, nothing special. I guess last night she did remind me for the twentieth time not to use expressions like 'you know,' 'real good,' and 'sort of.' But..."

Fran chimed in, "That's not what Mom *means*."

Mrs. Lindsay reached for her pack of Camels. She lit a cigarette, inhaled, exhaled, and spoke again. "Let's put it another way. Do you know what happens when a girl gets her period?"

"Period? No, I—I—guess I don't."

"My goodness, your mother must be very modest."

I stiffened. At least my mother didn't smoke. "Well, *I* happen to think she's wonderful!"

Mrs. Lindsay seemed not to hear. She handed me a thin pamphlet whose cover displayed a darling sketch of a swallowtail butterfly hovering over a gardenia. "I sent off for this especially for you. Why not browse through it while Fran and I go rustle up some snacks?"

I studied the cover. At the top it said, "A gift from the Modess Company." Modess! I recognized that word, all right: I'd last seen it inscribed under those pirouetting ladies in the women's magazines. The title read "WHAT EVERY GIRL NEEDS TO KNOW." Leafing through the pamphlet, my eyes lighted on picture after picture of sky-blue, feminine torsos, some seen from the front, some from the side. Inside each torso, I recognized various organs in contrasting white, connected to each other by what appeared to be plumbing pipes. Urgent arrows indicated which direction some mysterious substance—liquid, I assumed — was supposed to flow. Another illustration showed a willowy girl with a page boy, frowning in concentration, as she scribbled something on a large wall calendar. I read on until the walnut- raisin cookies and apple cider arrived. But try as I might, I just couldn't connect my own torso with all those complicated blue ones. But I did absorb the information that every gal's anatomy was destined to act in a certain way. I would not escape.

About a year later, returning from Garfield, I burst in through the kitchen door, feeling the usual happy relief at coming home. But where was my mother? I found her on the living room sofa, reading. Odd. She usually only allowed herself that luxury after dinner. Full of *joie de vivre*, she preferred the outdoors to the stuffy indoors.

"Sit down, Ruthie." We children knew that when she asked one of us to sit down with her, it always meant a serious topic was about to be broached.

As I sat down, my eyes fell on some curious objects on the round coffee table in front of us: something white and elastic, rather like the garter belt she wore to keep her stockings up, and beside it, a pastel pink carton, about the size of a cornflakes box but wider. It was labeled "Modess." Oh, no! Not again! Beside it lay a familiar-looking pamphlet inscribed, WHAT EVERY GIRL NEEDS TO KNOW. My mother, smiling, handed it to me.

She cleared her throat.

RUTH A. HANHAM

THE SUMMIT IS IN THE DOING

Ian announced he was going elk hunting. My husband was not commencing a negotiation about whose turn it was to do the fun stuff. No, he was simply telling me that the hunting season in Idaho had opened and that he, even though he wasn't a regular hunter, was going to Idaho for ten days with his two contractor clients.

"Elk hunting! Ten days!" I cried in alarm, "How on earth can we afford that?" Some months we could barely pay the electric bill.

Ian quickly backtracked to rationalize that his new buddies would likely be hiring him to design more spec houses. Going elk hunting was an investment in his startup architecture firm.

Well! I knew there was no way that was I going to stay home and mind our five small children while Ian roamed the Idaho wilderness and enjoyed convivial dinners of steak and whiskey. I loved the wilderness, too, and I needed a vacation as much as he did, probably more. I would find something memorable to do while he was gone. I would climb Mt. Whitney.

This was not a hair-brained departure from my normal life. When I was seventeen, I had gone on a Sierra Club Base Camp trip in the Palisades region where I had met a tall twenty-one-year-old named Ian. By the end of that summer of 1947, he and I had climbed six of the fifteen 14,000-foot peaks on the West Coast, and I had my heart set on ascending the remaining nine of these tallest peaks.

Mt. Whitney, at 14,495 feet, was the highest of the 14,000-ers. By 1962 I had already climbed it from the north by an unusual route up steep, slippery snow fields. That was venturesome compared to the normal ascent, a non-technical but grueling march up a long, steep trail with countless switchbacks. Still, the Whitney climbs that beckoned to me the most were those on the legendary, vertical East Face. I got a queasy thrill just thinking about the most direct one, a vertiginous rock climb with tricky spots dubbed the "Fresh Air Traverse" and the "Shaky-Leg Crack."

No, no. I dismissed that classic East Face climb from the realm of the possible for this weekend. We'd tackle the easier "Mountaineer's Route" which lay just north of the vertical route. We would still be on the East Face, but we'd have a long and eminently do-able scramble to the top. I envisioned the halcyon hour on the summit with my climbing companions. With the thin air singing over the granite blocks and climbing ropes coiled, we would nestle in the rocks, munch dried fruit, and identify the surrounding peaks. Even compared to steaks and whiskey, that would be heaven.

So, who would watch the kids, and who would this "we" be, these climbing companions in my idyllic hour on the summit? I grabbed the phone. Yes, our babysitter would corral the brood for a long weekend. Yes, my brother Dick was keen to go climbing. Yes, my fellow rock climbers and good friends Gail and Al Baxter would postpone a winemaking session and join us. Our climb now had two ropes of two persons each, perfect. We'd leave well before dawn on Saturday morning from

Berkeley and be on the trail by the early afternoon. Sunday we'd climb Whitney and get home at some wee hour Sunday night.

Impulsive dashes to the mountains were possible 1962. We lived in an era of mountain freedoms that we took for granted. Wilderness Permits and trailhead quotas had not yet been invented. We simply arrived, even at the highly popular Whitney trailhead, and started hiking. If we wished, we camped next to a lake, rather than one hundred feet away. With no need for a water filter, we drank the pure mountain water right out of lakes and streams. We hauled our food bags up trees to safety from marmots and chipmunks, and we never saw a marauding bear. All I had to do back then was pack our food and gear. After Ian departed for Idaho, I was preparing backpacking food: pouring oatmeal, raisins, dried milk, and the rest of our mountain cuisine into plastic bags. I was happy. I was going mountain climbing.

We drove down Highway 395 on the eastern side of the Sierra, branched off in the heat of the Owens Valley on the Mt. Whitney road, and climbed up the twists and turns to Whitney Portal and the welcome cool of aspen at 9500 feet elevation. It was an early September afternoon when we crunched into the parking area. We rushed to load our backpacks with our personal gear and the community supplies – food, cooking gear, and the climbing ropes – and started up the sandy, rocky main trail to Mt. Whitney. The east face of the Whitney massif towered in the west, promising a golden sunset "Alpine glow" a few hours hence. I felt a similar glow in my heart.

An indistinct foot trail angled from the main trail toward Pinnacle Pass. We took it and quickly were picking our way up easy ledges that led us to the lowest point on the ridge. Here we stopped to rest our backpacks on the granite rocks. As I leaned back and admired the darkening blue twilight overhead, I discerned a point of light that, yes, was moving slowly across the sky. What was it? I felt a flash of superstitious awe, akin to a tribesman in the highlands of Papua New Guinea, sighting an airplane for the first time. Flying saucer? Aliens? Then I realized, of course, it must be that new technological marvel, a satellite. We had hardly started our weekend, and already I had a memorable, even historic, moment to treasure.

Darkness was coming on. We had to get down to Iceberg Lake. Snow lay between the rocks on the north side of the pass, and the dropping temperature froze the slippery patches. We descended cautiously and reached a campsite in a spectacular spot on the shore. The lake was already starting to freeze, and an early snow lay on the ground. The cliffs of the east face of Mt. Whitney rose above us to the west.

Dick and I pitched our small tent. We pulled on down parkas and brewed hot soup and an instant rice supper. The darkness came fast since the days were already getting short. By flashlight we scrutinized the topographic map and the description of the climb in the Climber's Guide. The Mountaineers Route was second to third class, basically a long vigorous scramble using arms and legs. We would be ready to rope up in the steeper sections. The moon floated above. Dick played his harmonica and we sang a few camp songs, but it was very cold. We retreated to our sleeping bags.

Dawn broke. I had slept in my clothes and getting up was a simple matter of cinching my bra strap, abandoning the cozy warmth of my sleeping bag, and donning my icy boots. From my pack I fished a breakfast treat, a loaf of homemade nut bread. The crust bulged with nuts and raisins, but when I peeled back the wax paper, I sniffed the poisonous scent of cooking fuel. Ugh! A leaky canister of white gas in an outside pocket of my pack had obviously contaminated the bread. Oh well, coffee and hot oatmeal with raisins and brown sugar would be enough.

Dick pumped up the small Primus gas stove, primed the opening, and lit the fuel. The stove started with its normal sputter, followed by the usual rushing sound of burning white gas. Yay, coffee was coming. I imagined warming my fingers around my coffee cup. But it was not to be. The tiny Primus gave a mighty roar and a pillar of flame rose eight feet above the little stove. The Papua New Guinea tribesman could not have been more astonished than we were at this Biblical-seeming event. In our pre-caffeine state we gaped at the spectacle of our exploding cook stove.

Al finally muttered, "Put that in your memory book!" And I said, "Along with that great soup with leftover bacon and spring onions that we had in the Palisades?" And Gail said, "Right." Then we ate a cold breakfast cobbled from lunch materials.

Our camp was in chill shadow, but the sun was just touching the highest cliffs. We had to hustle if we expected to climb Mt. Whitney, return to the lake for our packs, climb back over Pinnacle Pass in daylight, and drive home to Berkeley. We cleaned up the camp and stowed lunches and water in our daypacks. I draped one of our two climbing ropes around my neck. We picked our way up the granite boulders until we reached the point at which the serious climbing up the Mountaineers Route started – or so we thought.

The granite rose steeply above us. Obviously it was time to rope up. We clustered on a narrow rock bench for a huddle about how to proceed. Dick suspected that the route was to our left, and Al declared that it circled to the right. Since Al had the most climbing experience, Dick deferred with, "You give it a try."

"Here goes." Al started up a wide crack. Gail paid out the rope and Al disappeared diagonally, out of view. Then the rope stopped moving upward. We waited. The rope gave a few twitches, but no call for "up rope." And then Al shouted that he was coming back down. When he rejoined us, he shook his head in frustration. His route had petered out in a smooth rock face.

I was eager to try our luck to our left. I secured the rope around my waist with a bowline, and Dick paid out the rope as I made my way across a slab to a promising series of broken rocks. Tucking one toe into a great foothold and gripping a handhold above my head, I wriggled my body up and over a bulge in the face. "Up rope," I yelled, and Dick fed me more rope. I climbed a few more yards and then my route, too, vanished in smooth rock. Wedging my body between two rocks, I assessed the steep rocks above. If we were hoping to find a simple scramble to the summit, this wasn't it. I shouted that I was climbing back down.

What to do? With dismay we concluded that we were not on the Mountaineer's Route. Our expected jaunt to the summit had metamorphosed into a demanding, technical rock climb. Time had slipped away, and we would have to give up climbing the mountain that day.

But it was a glorious day. The sun had risen in the sky, warming the cliffs and our chilled fingers. We had the entire mountain basin to ourselves. The thin mountain air moved gently over the rocks. From our perch on the granite bench we saw the Owens Valley far below to the east, shimmering dusty yellow in the distance. We sat on our granite thrones, opened our daypacks, and reveled in our usual trail lunch of cheese, salami, crackers, and dried fruit. Even though it looked a lot like breakfast.

Then it was time to retrace our steps and head home. We coiled the ropes and picked our way back down the jumble of boulders to the frozen lake. I stowed the blackened Primus stove in my pack as a souvenir of the pillar of flame. Maybe I could get a new safety valve. The return climb over Pinnacle Pass was a breeze with the afternoon's softened snow underfoot.

As we drove home, we talked about our thwarted climb.

"I wonder where the Mountaineer's Route went," said Dick, "Damn thing just disappeared."

"A complete mystery," said Al. "But we sure had a great flame show this morning. For a whole minute I thought we were in the same league as the Burning Bush."

"Don't forget the satellite on Pinnacle Pass," I said. "And if we're talking about memorable, I'll never forget that gassy loaf of nut bread and how good salami can taste for breakfast."

"Maybe next time we'll have leftover bacon, too," Gail joined in.

We turned off Highway 395 and climbed west up Tioga Pass, headed home. In the next days, I savored my memories of the camp songs at the frozen lake and our lunch on a granite throne. My emotional batteries had been recharged. Despite aching muscles and lack of sleep, I felt a loving patience for my children. Even the sunlight flooded in a golden way through the windows of our home – and, very possibly, my soul.

I was in this state when Ian came home from Idaho. The elk hunter returned triumphant. Steaks and whiskey had been consumed in quantity around the campfire; mountains and valleys had been tramped in successful stalking of elk. Many pounds of elk meat would soon be in our freezer.

"And so you see? The cost isn't much when you think of all the elk I brought home!"

Whoops. The cost wasn't much? My equanimity lurched. For Ian's infant architectural practice I had been functioning as the Everything Secretary and Bookkeeper. We had been living from architectural fee to architectural fee, supplemented by financial help from Ian's father, and I knew just how tight our finances were every month.

So, how many pounds of elk meat was that? I sharpened my pencil and added up Ian's costs – his share of the airplane ride to a landing strip, the packer and mules, and everything else. Then I divided the total by elk pounds. The result was quadruple the cost of the finest filet mignon at the local butcher store.

When I confronted Ian with my unassailable arithmetic, he quickly backed down from his silly rationalization. That was so satisfying that I found myself experiencing an emotional reset, and I conceded that my math was really an exercise in showing the impossibility of quantifying the unquantifiable. We couldn't possibly know how much Ian's architectural practice would benefit from his elk hunting trip. Nor could I quantify the value of my independent dash to climb Mount Whitney. Some forays are a gamble. Maybe you don't get to the summit. Maybe it doesn't matter.

KATE "CRICKET" POPE

SMITTEN AT THIRTEEN

At thirteen years old, in the eighth grade, I became smitten. He was a boy in the grade a semester ahead of mine. Greg was his name, although all the other kids called him Reeser, his last name. Greg was neither tall nor short, a little chunky, but not too much, with short blond hair. He was not particularly handsome, except to me.

I don't remember how I first encountered him. We wouldn't have been in a class together. In Sacramento's early 1960s, kids attended classes strictly by the grade they were in. The only classes that I took with mixed-grade students were Band and Home Economics. Greg played no musical instrument, nor did he plan to be a housewife. But I surely couldn't have missed noticing him during recess, lunch, or passing by him in the school hallways: he was loud and boisterous. He attracted other kids' attention.

I was too shy then to have made any first move, or even to bring attention to me. I was far from bold in matters of the heart. And what would have caused him to approach me? We ran in different social circles and rarely did kids in my school have the gumption to step outside the comfort of their crowd. But he was not one bound to societal norms. No one could tell Greg what to do or how to be. Would he have stopped in the hall, turned to me, and said, "Hey, you're cute! I'd like to meet you." His eagerness would have made a nice memory! But no, that didn't happen. I know, for he never returned the fervor I had for him to me.

But in whatever way I met him, on that first time and every time thereafter, my thirteen-year-old heart was walloped by his presence.

In those days I had a lucky sweatshirt: good things happened to me just by wearing it. I won many Ping-Pong and Canasta games one summer with that sweatshirt. At school dances, boys asked me to dance. But caution warned me not to overuse its magic; so, I saved it for special times. And here was the opportunity; I would put on my lucky sweatshirt when I was likely to run into Greg. Again and again, it didn't work. I put my powerless sweatshirt away.

Somehow, we did meet and became friends, although I'd say it was an imbalanced friendship. I was smitten and had surrendered to that first puppy love feeling, knowing the object of my infatuation was unattainable and even unreasonable. Just seeing him lifted my day and fed my fantasies. Yet, like riding the rollercoaster's ascent, I should have anticipated its inevitable descent. Soon enough my unreciprocated longing turned against me.

This unrequited love that had appeared at the start of my teenage years persisted for long after. It shaped my self-esteem and my expectations of success in personal relationships.

In the ninth grade, Greg moved to another school on the outskirts of Sacramento. No longer would I walk the halls feeling my knees shake as we'd pass each other. Nor would I unexpectedly run into him at some party, exchange a few companiable remarks, or even ride home in the same car with him, both of us squeezed into the back seat. I yearned to repeat the experience of feeling the press of his thigh on mine, his arm, with no space for it, slung over the back of the seat behind me, and his torso pushed next to mine, we were so close. Electricity ran through these touch points, making thunder of my heartbeat he surely could sense. I had little experience with boys and even less with sexual feelings. Those were just boys trying to take advantage, while I fought them off. I would have succumbed, I imagined, had he made a move. But he never did.

I didn't have a real boyfriend during my high school years. There were a few dates, some platonic relationships, other unreciprocated infatuations, and that was all.

After Greg moved away, I'd run into him, unexpectedly, about twice a year. The surge of passion he triggered in my body became familiar: racing heart, jelly legs, shallow breathing, hot flashes. Symptoms that, at my now advanced age, could be diagnosed as atrial fibrillation, low blood pressure, asthma, and hormonal imbalances. As a teenager, these physical reactions put me in an altered state, outside of myself and the banality of daily life.

On a few of those impromptu encounters during my Greg-deprived high school years, Greg asked me out: to a movie and once to take a drive for cheesecake at a restaurant thirty miles away. These were not official or formal dates; they were offers for mutual companionship. I felt a sweet rapport during the times we were alone together. He had no reason to boast, act the jokester, or wear a social façade. He was just himself, authentic, thoughtful, sober. There was a friendly ease in each other's company. By concentrating on every moment with him, I stretched and savored those times, enough to tide me over until our next encounter, which I knew would come.

Following high school, Greg joined the Army, was sent to Vietnam, and served several tours there. I wrote him occasional letters, with no mention of my, or his, feelings. I placed no demands on this soldier. Rather, I hoped these letters would serve as a connection to a life he had left behind, that there were people from his past who thought of him. He wrote me, choosing only mundane topics, keeping, I assumed, the horror of his experience hidden in between his words. These white spaces stirred my imagination.

I entered the working world and attended college after high school. My social consciousness awakened with the growing anti-war sentiment, even in conservative Sacramento. But I could place no blame on Greg for the evils of war, even if he had enlisted. I stored his letters in an empty red and white Marlboro cigarette carton.

When he came to see me a few times in between tours, I assumed he did so to show his gratitude for my letters and for the Christmas box of cookies I had sent. I didn't care what his motives were; I reveled in the old feelings he secretly stirred within me.

In those interludes between battle, Greg was charged with notifying families of soldiers killed in the war that their sons were not coming home. And how, I asked, does that make you feel, how can you bear it? He closed up, did not let me come inside, and changed the subject.

By the time I was in my twenties, I had lost track of him. I was left wondering if his name was inscribed on the Vietnam War Memorial, or whether he lived on, got married, raised a family, or...?

The cigarette carton followed me with every household move I made in those years of my youth—until it became time to purge my teenage attachment to fantasy. It was an impulsive act, I know, to burn Greg's letters; an act I regretted moments after they were gone. And then came relief. I threw the empty Marlboro carton into the dying flames.

VIVIAN PISANO

IS IT TIME?

Is it time? Should I start looking for my phone in the refrigerator? Are the bananas in the suitcase? It is becoming evident to me that I am prone to flakiness. I don't fear dementia, but this flakiness, I have seen before.

My mother...let's call her Jane...couldn't keep track of, or seem to care about details.

She got *where* and *how* mixed up and forgot what she said to whom.

As she got older her flakiness got worse. She forgot to tell me that my uncle died. I found out six months after the fact.

She couldn't remember which of her five kids hated meatloaf and which one hated fish.

She was cavalier with her medications; too much, too little, morning or night; *Eh, same diff* she would say.

She drove like she was at the bumper cars. Running over the curb. *So, no big deal,* she would say. Bumping into a pole she would announce cheerfully; *Well I guess we're here!*

When her frequent falls upset me, *Eh, Don't let it throw ya.* Time and again my brother got the call. He had to drop what he was doing, to go pick her up off the floor.

She called me to untangle financial snafus she didn't understand.

Jane's mother... let's call her Grandma... had ten granddaughters. When talking to us, she would use all our names. It was a list of baby boomer girls: Susiepattyellendebbienancygaildianekathymary...she kept going until she got it right. We always knew who she was talking to, though.

I'm Linda, I would smile, *Jane's oldest.*

Oh you! I know who you are, don't be so smart, she would grouch. Grandma's grouch was always worse than her bite.

These days, I am accruing something of a record myself.

—Recently, my granddaughter found my phone buried in the linen closet.

—I melted a plastic spatula on a hot griddle pan. It stretched off the griddle like mozzarella.

—I routinely open the cupboard door when I am looking for something in the freezer and vice versa. The two doors are right next to each other and similar in size and color. It is only a matter of time before there is a bag of chips in the freezer and ice cream in the cupboard.

—Sometimes, I notice trails on the floor. Who put that ravioli on the floor? When did I spill that coffee?

—Twice now, I have brushed my teeth with facial cleanser and it is bitter, let me tell you. The two tubes are markedly different in size, so how do I explain that?

—I have forgotten parties or dinner plans. Or went on the wrong day.

—How many times have I left the house with the important tickets, mailings or packages still on the counter?

—I, too, have dented my fender, backing into the rocks along a friend's driveway.

—On a family visit to Boulder, it was several days before noticing that I had been washing dishes from a bottle clearly labeled HAND SOAP. I hope no one noticed. Also, I pinned a perfect ballerina bun atop my granddaughter, my best ever. But she had specifically said NOT a ballerina bun. Somehow, I hadn't heard the NOT. She wanted a messier, lower knot that day.

—Alas, it continues. In the past month I headed to engagements on the wrong day... TWICE. It is not that I haven't written them down, it was just that the difference between Monday and Tuesday had alluded me those particular days.

Meanwhile, I wonder what an observer would make of my daily Modus Operandi. I do a little on the crossword, then I gather a little laundry, then I sit at my desk and put all the desk errands aside for another time, letting them pile up until they become irrelevant, then clean something else, then I email a friend, settle in with a book, then I take a nap... and so forth. It is a chain of partial tasks. This used to be called Attention Deficit Disorder. As a teacher, I could spot it a mile away. I began to think it was contagious and that I caught it from the kids. Now, I have a gizmo on my wrist that tells me when to stand, gives me an exercise credit for walking to the next room and reminds me to breath. These scattered actions are now called Wellness.

In years to come, should I need closer guidance, I will cooperate. My goal is to be the sweet, appreciative type, not the cantankerous, scary elder. I have met them both. A nice, small apartment with good light, and a water view - is all I'll need. I will sign a promise right now.

LINDA SONDHEIMER

A BLACK-TIE GALA: What I Think of You and What I Think You Think of Me

Oh, my. My comment that Medicare is good for the country turns you into stone. Up until now we've been chatting about sports – of which I know almost nothing: golf (I've read one book about it, *A Good Walk Spoiled*); basketball (a good sports fanatic friend advised me, "just talk about players' injuries and everyone will believe you're an expert!") and baseball (it draws you because your mother had been a softball star who wanted you to be either an athlete or a scholar). High school left you hating academics and your just-below-varsity talent for athletics disappointed you, but a professor at a small college helped you love politics. Money, you said, you're good at making money.

You and I are seated together in a ballroom beneath hotel chandeliers eating rubber chicken for me, surf and turf for you, because you're a thousand dollar per plate paying patron, and I for charity's sake must make an appearance as a benefactor. But I'll keep you guessing why I'm here. Uncomfortable, you look uncomfortable sitting next to me, someone who doesn't look like you. Relax, man. I'm not an exotic animal from Asia. I'm wearing an elegant spaghetti-strap silk gown in elegant aubergine. My mother's fox fur cape is draped over the back of my chair. When you think I'm not looking, you like stroking it; and my tiara dazzles you. You can tell me that you like what I'm wearing if you're at a loss for something to say.

Uh-oh. Your eyes are cold. Your demeanor is smug. Yup. You're suspicious of squinty eyes and yellow skin. You look angry. You're feeling angry that someone like you, owner of three yachts and a personal friend of the President of the U.S. of A., has to sit next to me, someone who reminds you of a dragon lady who likes torturing her daughters, whipping them and chaining them to the wall until they've worn their fingers to the bone practicing the piano and finishing their advanced placement math homework. I'm not happy either, and I'm tired of answering your boring questions, "Where do you come from?" "What does your father do?" I'm tired of explaining I was born here, just like you. I won't tell you that my family probably has a longer history than yours in America. My family can trace its genealogy all the way back to ten thousand A.D. Can yours?

Ah, dessert's here and it's time for the speeches. Your mouth drops when the M.C. introduces the founders and I stand up with the others. You're surprised! Great. You didn't expect a woman, least of all a petite, unathletic-looking, Asian-American woman to be so closely involved in an annual two-day men's college basketball tournament. I'm a federal lobbyist who helps rich companies get richer. I won't tell you that I helped establish both the foundation and the basketball tournament to make myself feel better. I want to help kids that "your kind" (your words, not mine) doesn't want to help. Because you don't want to pay taxes, the children I want to help are deprived of health and education. Can you guess that I'm using basketball to help you give back what you take from them?

While you think only of bonding with the boys, I know the tournament is a million-dollar money pit. I won't bore you with the fact that I am the one who came up with the idea of the gala – it pays for the tournament's expenses (over one million dollars) *and* the essential half million dollars our foundation donates to the city's at-risk children. You pay one thousand dollars a ticket to sit right next to the arena floor. That was also my idea. To be seen as top dog paying top dollar. To be up close and personal. To catch every one of the players' sweaty but graceful balletic moves.

I know all about you. I know your mistress has enough diamond bracelets; I know about your newest billion-dollar estate, your fast cars, your favorite sports teams. I won't tell you that I leave my body when you ask me, "Where are you from? And when did you come to the United States?" You try to be nice to me saying "You speak English so well." Even Orrin Hatch doesn't assume I'm an immigrant. He talked about poetry, music and good food. He listened, asked questions about what I love, like and hate. I don't know if he's genuinely tolerant, he's still a politician. He needs my company's contribution to his election campaign. At least, at that breakfast we laughed, and that's why the next time we met he remembered my name. That's also why he's a long-time Senator and you're not even a venerable VIP.

During the entertainment you whisper in my ear you like my gown and jewelry. I commiserate with you about injuries that the Georgetown team suffered this year. But I don't disclose what I think because I want to bless the city's children with your money.

ELEANOR LEW

FINAGLING A FENCE

It wasn't a dark and stormy night: it was a late summer afternoon when I had to remove my perimeter fence, leaving a third of my small property exposed to the world. That world, a wooded cul de sac with only a few nearby houses, is mostly fox, raccoon, opossum, deer, and coyote by night, and dog walkers, joggers, and walking groups by day. Plus, a long line of characters, not always savory, that this quiet, leafy cul de sac seems to beckon.

I didn't want to take down my deer fence: its removal seemed to serve no purpose. My fence sat on a small slice of a large piece of undeveloped land that includes a wide, earthen walking path. That path is also an EBMUD (East Bay Municipal Utility District) easement. This easement means no structures can be built up the walking path, although it could become a driveway or a road. The removal of my fence would not allow the walking path to become wider or more useful. I also knew the absence of my fence would not make the property more saleable, as it had not sold in the past when there was no fence. But I had no choice: a certified, registered letter from the owner's attorney directed me to remove the fence. I expected I'd feel exposed, maybe even a little scared, but my house has an alarm, is not on a busy street, and I had lived here for two years without that fence.

The owner's father had given me permission to install that fence. That was in 2014. He didn't ask where I planned to install the fence, nor what kind of fence it might be. He was surprisingly laissez faire. His property, which includes the walking path, is 1.64 acres of raw, undeveloped land, much of it steep and studded with thickets of poison oak, oak trees, and eucalyptus. That gorgeous, wide walking path, bounded by thick trunked oaks, has been used by countless people and their dogs for at least sixty years, since the tracks of the Sacramento Northern Railway were removed in 1957. I had merely asked to install "a deer fence (to keep out deer, varmints, and vagrants) on part of your property." I had also asked to buy that slice of his property. He said yes to the fence, as long as I'd remove it when asked, and said nothing about the arc of land. I figured I'd remove the fence when there was a good reason, like an approved building permit.

Fast forward to 2021. One of my neighbors had asked me for the owner's phone number, and a few days later told me that the phone had been disconnected. Uh oh: the owner had been in his 90s. Shortly after that, another neighbor emailed me photos of three trees that had been marked 10, 11, and 12 in red spray paint. Alarmed, I went to see for myself, remembering the surveyors I had seen the previous week, guessing that they had marked the trees. Yes, I conclude the owner of the large property has died. Did he leave heirs?

I walk up the dirt steps that cut into the owner's property, open my gate to the walking path, and see an orange "2" painted on the CalTrans (California Department of Transportation) fence. Oh! So the owner had more than one property! Maybe that's where trees #1-9 are. Not knowing whether the numbers mean these trees are slated for removal or for protection, I admire them anew, photograph them, then walk further down the walking path, and up the slippery, oak-leafed slope behind Marie Way, into the expansive clearing, then past the circular depression where I spot trees 14 & 15, but never tree 13, thinking maybe it's bad luck to use the number 13, I don't know. Then I carefully make my way down behind the eagle-nesting tallest eucalyptus we've dubbed the "Mother Euc," emerging through the CalTrans property to the cul de sac and my house.

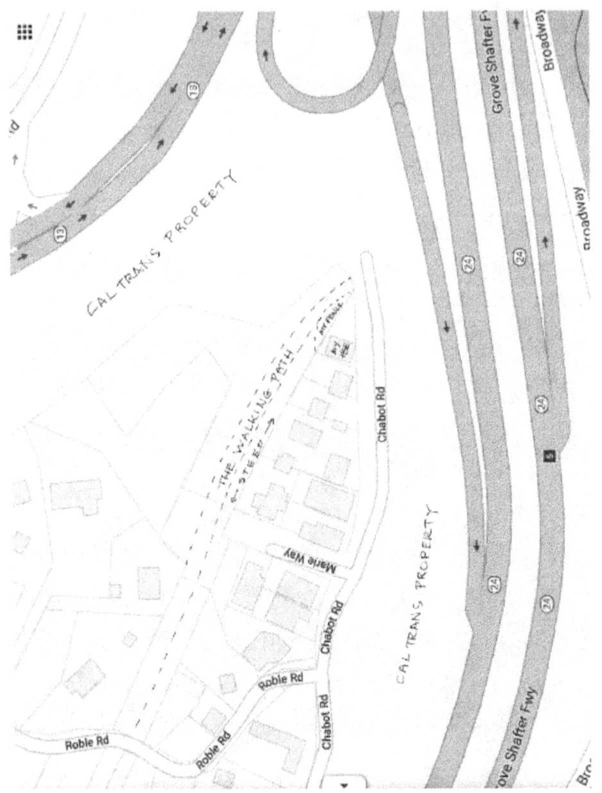

Map: My house, my fence, and the walking path

Eventually, neighbor Chris and I arrange to meet the son, the executor of his father's estate, in my patio. Spread before us is a survey map of the property, revealing it as a strange Y shaped piece of land bifurcated by someone else's raw land. I ask for a copy of the survey. The son says it's the sole property of Summit Engineering. The son hopes "the neighbors" will buy the property to extend their lot lines into the walking path. I hope so too, but soon realize that the back yards of my neighbors' houses are too steep to access the walking path: I'm the only property that easily abuts the walking path. Try as I might, none of them is interested.

While the future of the property is unclear, I see other signs that my neighborhood is changing. Jen and Emily and their two darling daughters just moved: now their house is up for sale. And my next door neighbor Sharon, after forty years on this street, has moved into assisted living. Soon her house too will be for sale. My dream world is mutating, its future uncertain.

One day it occurs to me that maybe I could buy the property. Then I could do a lot line adjustment for the wedge of land between my fence and my property line, and sell the remainder: my sliver of 1,327 s.f. won't make a dent in the total 71,439 s.f. I call my financial guy. Curiously, eagerly, audaciously I ask;

"Dean, can you issue me a loan for $600,000 cash?" (That was so much fun!)

"Sure. Probably more.".

"Terms?

"3.095% interest only loan, principal payable at the end of ten years. Annual interest is $18,000. Paid monthly that's $1,500."

Gulp! I'd have to sell stock, incurring a hefty 23% capital gains tax. Two years… Maybe I could swing this for two years.

Stoked! I send an email offering to buy the property for $600,000 cash. The owner counters with $650,000. I hold firm. The next week I hike the steep, slippery property with him and Maurice, my design-build specialist friend. I play chess weekly with Maurice's 97-year-old father. It's not so much that Maurice owes me, but our interests align. I learn to recognize the property boundaries. Maurice then lines up an architect-developer to walk the property. Conclusion? Yes, it's a difficult property, my fence is immaterial. Chris locates the prior listings of the property: It didn't sell in 2003 and in 2006 when the property was doubly accessible, with more development potential because the two interlocking properties were offered together, enabling one route up to the building sites and another route down.

By now, I am now fully enmeshed in the details of the property. Most of my waking moments I'm visualizing where to place the access road to the buildable sites. I'm trying to learn what a developer/buyer needs to know so I can resell the property, learning some required "due diligence" for completely raw land with no roads, no sewers, no water, no lighting, no electricity, no grading, nada. I make multiple phone calls to the Fire Department to learn fire engine turn-around requirements, leaving voice mail messages. I suspect that if the two properties didn't sell back then, now when it's just one property, with only one way to the building sites, it probably won't sell in the two years I can afford to carry the loan. But I proceed a little further with my "due diligence," trying to learn every problem and its solution to promote its resale. I conclude again and again that it probably won't sell in two years. I withdraw my informal offer. Two weeks later I receive a call back from Oakland Fire's vegetation management officer, who searches the regulations and discovers that it's up to the Fire Commissioner to determine the required turn-around. No wonder it's hard to advise buyers about raw land with such an important detail not set by the code!

Soon after withdrawing my offer, the son's attorney sends me that certified registered letter, giving me one month to remove my fence. Plus, the letter also states that I can no longer walk on the property! What? Will he have cameras installed to catch me? My two cats know no property lines. When it's time to bring them inside at night, I call or bodily retrieve them, especially Goldie who likes to sleep in the tangle of Cape Honey Suckle just beyond my property line.

I contact my real estate agent Sara. We write a legal offer to buy the little wedge of property. I offer four times more per square foot than he's asking for the rest of the site. Meanwhile I scramble to find a land surveyor who will stake my true property line. I make countless phone calls, leaving voice mail messages, filling out online forms of inquiry. Only one firm responds. That one call back is the result of a personal referral from landscape architect Walter Hood's project managers. Walter and I know each other from UC Berkeley's College of Environmental Design: our studios are in the same complex. After a month, my offer is denied.

I'm now into my third month of nearly full-time day-dreaming and questioning. I still don't know what right the public might have to the walking the path. Chris is sure 150 people per week walk the path. I estimate about half that many. Neither of us were going to sit there with a clip board or a clicker from dawn to dusk, no matter the weather.

In September, the son builds a fence blocking the Marie Way end of the walking path. Why I have no idea. A few days later he places posts and a chain at the cul de sac, with a brass plate embedded in concrete citing Civil Code 1088, advising people they need permission to walk on his property. To what end are these restrictions? It's probably all about liability insurance. To my knowledge, no one has filed suit in sixty years. Is it supposed to make the land more attractive to future buyers? I ask around about his real estate agent. "Oh him! He's the bad boy of Oakland raw land" cites one friend, a realtor.

Doesn't the public have a right to continue to use this path after sixty years of use? The blocking of the path makes me remember the adage that "property is king." Meaning that individual rights prevail. Just like the anti-vaxxers and anti-maskers in their claim of freedom, where the individual reigns, the public be damned. Meanwhile, I'm thinking there must be some rights vested by historical usage. I'm not financially well-heeled, nor am I part of an active group with a treasury like the surfers with Surfrider Foundation backing them up over the closure of Martin's Beach, a case that was pending for ten years. I'm just one person who knows few of the path walkers by name.

My fence came down by the deadline. The view is so beautiful! My fence did not obscure the view, but it was easy to look just to the fence line. In the foreground, you can see my gracefully curved cedar and gravel steps centering the view, a view flanked by redwood and oak trees. In the middle ground, the slope flattens out. That's the walking path: you can't see it from where I'm standing near my three beehives. And beyond, you see the golden-brown California hills with their towering eucalyptus. It's a classical three-part composition, a stage set of foreground, middle ground, and background. I admire the view. Such a shame to block the path!

I re-think my fence plans: maybe I won't re-install my deer fence along my legal property line. Even though "deer, varmints, and vagrants" are still a reality, my property line might not be its best placement. For weeks, my quiet moments are spent visualizing a variety of fence placements: less here, more there, until my sister insists: you need some security at the end of the road where you're all by yourself. She's right: I just won't continue my fence along my patio edge: it's too unsightly for this indoor-outdoor house.

My next big surprise was receiving an email from my City Council member's staff, who had consulted with various state and local officials about the property. She advised me to send a "demand letter" with signatures from neighbors who have used the walking path for more than five years, claiming a "prescriptive easement." I'm off and running, contacting neighbors, drafting a letter, collecting signatures. Yesterday I sent a certified letter to the son, a copy to his attorney, with thirty-six signatures and the number of years each has walked the path.

Forget the fence! Let's save the walking path!

MARYLY SNOW

A TREE IN THE DARK

Aside from planning a simple dinner with her grown kids, she had avoided all the trappings of Christmas this year. Since Thanksgiving, Jane had been dealing with breast cancer. On this late afternoon, she went to the second breast surgeon for her opinion on diagnosis and what to do. The afternoon fell away as she sat in the clean, well-lighted, well-spaced waiting room where only one other patient sat and was soon called for a treatment. Watching the patient move across that room, toward that door, she shuddered, supposed x-rays and radiation and god knows what. The other patient moved slowly through it.

She practiced meditation then and surrendered to the waiting and the fact that *this* had to come first. There were no social events anyway due to the pandemic, no one to meet for Friday night dinner, no Book Group gathering with wine and cheese except virtually on Zoom, the new social network.

Cancer. These people behind the desk, behind the plastic shield, behind the door that leads to the surgeon's examination and conference rooms, they deal with cancer patients day in and day out, she thought. She felt awe for their skills and dedication. It gave her patience. Due to COVID, there were no magazines with inspiring articles about recovery. But she didn't care. There was just the appointment and the hope to get it out ASAP.

"I thought I was bullet proof," she had told her old friend who had been in steady chemo for nearly a year now.

"I'm so sorry," her friend had replied.

The surgeon was a highly respected specialist in breast cancer. She had seen her during a slight scare 15 years before. During the initial appointment this time, the doctor had taken so much time to really understand her overall health picture. Impressive, had thought Jane, but oh my how she has aged, I suppose I have too. Now, she tried to focus on the sketch the doctor was drawing to show the diagnosis and on the unfamiliar words like Hormone Receptors—that's good, then, she surmised. As breast cancers go, Jane appeared to be getting the best of a bad situation.

"We can't hope to schedule your surgery before the end of the year. This is the rush time for breast cancer." Odd, thought Jane, covering her disappointment. "That's why you had to wait so long for this appointment. We can go ahead with the breast MRI. They'll schedule that on your way out. And again, I'm sorry you had to wait so long."

"No, no. It's fine. You all are dealing with *cancer.*"

The appointment slip grasped in her hand, she headed out the large glass doors to the parking garage. It was dark. She was hungry. She felt cold.

As she started up the car, she announced "I'm going to order a tree! I don't care what it costs."

Some warmed up Mediterranean fish and rice sat beside the computer as she googled Christmas

Tree Delivery and found she could get one. Maybe even tonight. How weird and wonderful. Her heart pounded faster as she put in the credit card information. She thought of her father and their trips to the Christmas tree lot together, walking around and critiquing the trees until she was fully satisfied and then the negotiations he would have with the proprietor, all in good humor in the dark, close to closing time.

She chewed with satisfaction as she thought of the tree in a truck somewhere, coming to her – maybe tonight. She retrieved one box of decorations from the garage. It wouldn't be a large tree. Turned on her recording of the evening's PBS NewsHour. Christ, a mutant strain now in England. And we're not even vaccinated against this one. She sighed, switched it off, and cleaned the kitchen.

Near 9 o'clock, she was sure that the tree was not coming tonight. She began to undress for a hot bath when a heavy footstep came up the stairs and she heard a firm rap at the door. She had left the porch light on in case.

This big young guy, about thirties or forty, said he wanted to show the tree to her and see if it was all right. She grabbed a jacket and followed him down the stairs to the driveway.

"Just a minute. I'll get it."

He went to the truck parked on the street and brought back a huge tree. "It must be seven feet high!" she exclaimed.

"Oh, no, sorry, I don't have room for a tree like that."

He said, "I can saw off the bottom for you."

She paused. "Hmmm. Yes. But then it would be four feet high and five feet wide," she pointed out, frowning. "See what I mean?"

"Well, how do you like the wreath?" He was tall, dark, and strong. And wanted to please.

"The wreath is fine. Very fresh. Nice." Her surge of hope and enthusiasm began to drain as he carried the big tree back to the truck. Then he returned.

"There's another tree in the truck. The people weren't home. And they didn't want me to leave it. Maybe you could have that one?" He went and got it.

An outstanding tree. A Douglas fir with those wonderful needles and a perfect shape. Kind of big for her room.

"Could you trim it?" He called his boss.

"You can have it for the same price as what you ordered."

"Sold!" She hadn't begun to worry about how she would get it set up when he said,

"I'll put it in a temporary stand for you, too."

"Really? Could you? No, oh, wait. I have one." Her feet were light as she let herself into the garage and stretched to the shelf where the tree stand waited.

"What's your name?" she asked as she carried the stand back to him.

"Nick."

"I'm Jane, Nick. Nice to know you."

He grinned and slapped his gloves together. She wanted to reach out and shake his hand. But no one was doing that anymore.

"First, he said, "Let's figure out where you want the bottom cut."

They made it a nice height about 5 ½ feet tall. Then he sawed off some floppy branches that would have hit the floor. He carried the tree inside and placed it in the tree stand. She held it tight while he adjusted it and made it just right.

When he stood back to admire it, he seemed to light up the room with his generous smile and warm, deep voice, "Now, that's a good tree."

Clearly this was a temporary job for the holidays. "What do you usually do?" she asked, as he placed the tree in front of the window.

He had a good job as a Cadillac mechanic, but they had cut back due to the pandemic.

She handed him some cash and thanked him profusely, "Nick, you have brought the spirit of Christmas here tonight! Thank you, thank you."

He accepted her gratitude and the money naturally, as if it was all as he expected it to be. She waved goodbye and closed the door.

She swept up the needles, put the branches on the porch, and watered the tree. She opened the box of decorations and pulled out the shiny, old Christopher Radko snowman with the pink ribbon on its breast and hung it on the tree. For tonight, it would reign there by itself. Then she started singing "Oh Tannenbaum" and danced around the floor. And was happy.

KAREN GRASSLE

MY CANINE ADVENTURES

I'm hanging onto my daddy's hand and being super careful not to slip on the slushy sidewalk or fall onto the packed gray snow heaped on both sides. I can tell that my daddy is happy because he is walking with an extra little bounce. We are on our way to visit my aunt and uncle on this cold and sunny winter day in the Bronx, New York in 1944.

As we pass an empty lot, I notice a big brown dog wandering far away. Whenever I see a dog, I get scared, just like my mommy. This dog doesn't seem to notice us. "Phew," I think, "Maybe we can sneak by." But just then my daddy starts to whistle and call to the dog, and the dog looks right at us.

"Daddy, don't call the dog! I'm afraid of dogs!

He gives me a surprised look, throws his head back laughing, and then whistles and calls again. Now the dog runs toward us, and here come two more dogs. I must hide before they get any closer. Where can I go? I pull my hand away from Daddy's so that I can hide behind him. I see an opening in the back of his coat, get under, shut my eyes, and wait for the dogs to go away. When I hear my daddy's deep rumbly voice, I dare to open my eyes and peek down. I see many dog legs circling around us and hear my daddy talking calmly and quietly—to the dogs.

With hindsight, I think my dad was bemused by my fear. He grew up in a village near Kraków, Poland, where dogs commonly roamed the streets and he had a pet dog of his own. No daughter of his would be afraid of dogs! If that was his intention, it was lost on five-year-old me.

Twenty-two dog-fearing years later, I see a girl, who looks about five years old, holding a woman's hand as they walk down a North Berkeley street. When a dog approaches them, the girl recoils and looks frightened. The woman scoops her up, ignores the dog, and talks calmly and quietly to the child. *How lovely*, I think, recalling the 1944 incident with my father, *this parent is taking the child's fear seriously and talking to her about it.* I decide on the spot that I must get a dog so that I can get over my fear of dogs and, at the same time, teach my children not to be afraid of them.

Soon after, my husband George and I learn that someone in our neighborhood has a litter of puppies they are giving away. We walk over with five-year-old Danny and three-year-old Jackie in tow and come home with an adorable tiny tan Terrier-mix puppy.

Cobbie is high-strung with a piercing high-pitched bark and is always underfoot. Much as we try to housebreak him, he leaves little puddles and piles of poop all around the house. I reach my breaking point when he leaves a pile on my pillow. Livid, I announce to George, "This is too much! A five-year-old, a three-year-old, and a puppy are too much for me. We'll have to part with one!"

A few days later, while George is walking Cobbie, he meets an elderly woman whose Terrier had recently died. She is so smitten with our puppy and we are so ready to find Cobbie a new home that our pet soon becomes hers.

Thanks to Cobbie, I no longer fear dogs, my children are comfortable with them, and our elderly neighbor is ecstatic. George and I consider Cobbie a successful short-term experiment.

Four years later, Danny and Jackie start advocating for a dog. They promise to help take care of it, and the four of us study dog breeds. We conclude that a Keeshond would be perfect for us for no other reason than its adorable resemblance to raccoons! We locate a breeder nearby and become the proud owners of a Keeshond puppy. Her pedigree papers refer to her as Lady, meaning female. Since she looks very elegant in her fluffy aura of gray and white fur, we adopt Lady as her name. Mimicking Bob Dylan's song, "Lay Lady Lay," that is all the rage, our mantra soon becomes a sing-song, "Stay Lady Stay!"

After a few dog-training classes we happily manage to housebreak and socialize Lady. Sadly, we can't teach her to come when we call her. When she doesn't come, Danny and Jackie chase her. That's how we end up training her to run away when we call her. We are now living in a cul-de-sac in Hayward, and we often run laps around the end of the road and up and down the quiet street in pursuit of Lady.

Keeshonds are shedding machines. Lady's overcoat is long, and her legs are relatively short. Branches and leaves cling relentlessly to her fur, requiring frequent brushing. Over time, we collect bags and bags of her soft fur for an artist friend who uses it in her woven pieces. All the vacuuming, brushing, and chasing make Lady a high-maintenance dog. Yet she is our darling and when she dies in old age, we chalk up another somewhat successful dog experience.

By the time I'm approaching fifty, we are settled in the Oakland Hills, and I am ready for a long-legged, short-furred dog that will be the perfect companion for jogging on trails in the redwoods. Danny and Jackie are Dan and Jack now, young adults on their own, and so it's entirely up to George and me to pursue our third adventure in dog ownership.

But what kind? We love the elegant grace and the floppy ears of the Rhodesian Ridgebacks we see on our jogging trails. Everything we read about this breed confirms our conviction that this is now the dog of choice for us. This time we opt to forego pedigree and instead list our request for a Ridgeback puppy at numerous shelters. When we finally hear from the San Francisco ASPCA shelter that they have a Rhodesian Ridgeback puppy for us, we zip over to find an adorable, velvety brown six-month-old male waiting for us. Even though his ridge isn't visible yet, his papers say Rhodesian Ridgeback Mix. His ears droop in the classic Ridgeback way. We can't be happier.

Our puppy makes curious singing sounds, and so we name him Gershwin. As he matures, the long-awaited ridge never comes in, and his adorable droopy ears, one by one, stand up and give him a particularly menacing look. His head and chest grow disproportionately large. Much to our horror, Gershwin looks more like a Pit Bull than a Rhodesian Ridgeback. He would have been better named a *Pit Bull Mix*. Even so, we've grown attached to this sweet but frightening looking dog.

We take Gershwin to dog training classes where we try very hard to convince him that we do not require his fierce protection from other dogs. He cannot be convinced. We try private sessions with a trainer who specializes in difficult dogs. She tells us, "*Never* take him off leash where there are other dogs around, and *always* carry a mixture of half white vinegar and half water in a spray bottle." She directs us to spray Gershwin's snout at any hint of aggression to disorient him just long enough for us to drag him off before he goes fully berserk. Gershwin grows to weigh ninety pounds, has a ferocious bark, and consistently becomes vicious at the sight of any other animal, be it chipmunk, squirrel, dog, or horse. On one of our walks at the San Leandro Marina, the sight of a chipmunk sends him into such a sudden lurch on the leash that it knocks me off my feet. The only animal who has the upper hand with him is our cat. They hang out together peacefully until she teases him into a friendly chase and then scampers up a tree, leaving Gershwin howling helplessly far below.

My father, who has a special fondness for Gershwin, starts calling him "Gootchie." George and I adopt the nickname, and I opt to transform it into "Gucci." What could be more ironic than such a high-end name for such a low-end mutt.

When friends come to visit, they often say, "You don't seem like the sort of people who would own a Pit-Bull!"

We reply, "Well, the fact is we're not, yet we do. You see, Gucci happened to us because we were so naive about the meaning of the word *mix*. But nothing to fear; he's lovely with people."

I avoid popular trails where Gucci might encounter other dogs. When we chance upon a horse and rider on a narrow back trail, Gucci becomes so deranged that the only way I can control him is to sit on him. How ridiculous I feel sitting on my lowly mad Gucci while the elegant horse and rider saunter by! After such incidents, I think briefly of returning Gucci to the shelter. But there's no way that could happen. He's our dog. When grandchildren become part of our lives, George and I become hyper-vigilant out of fear that Gucci will turn on them. Nothing of the sort ever happens. But when he dies in old age just before ruining ours, we are as relieved as we are sad. Now that we have grandchildren we are done with having pets, or so we think.

Mokie comes into our lives gradually. Our son Dan has carefully selected her as the ideal dog for his children, and for several years, she visits us along with our grandchildren. She is an adorable Springer Spaniel of medium size with symmetrical black and white markings, a freckled snout and floppy ears. Her coat is as soft as silk, nothing sticks to it, and she does not shed. Best of all, she has a delightful curiosity about other dogs. Her default setting is friendliness. We adopt her fondly as our grand-dog.

As the grandchildren become independent young adults, Mokie spends more and more time with George and me. Fully retired, we can dote on her while everyone else is away at work or at school. She lives with Dan several weekends a month. He showers her and returns her to us exuding clean dog fragrance. We share all grooming and medical expenses with Dan, and he takes her when we're traveling; a perfect arrangement all around.

George and I are now in our eighties, and Mokie is our devoted companion. She hates to be left alone, and so during the first eighteen months of the Covid pandemic, when we rarely leave our house, she is in her element. Our lives are so routinized that Mokie can anticipate our every move. After lunch, we all take a nap before the shared high point of every single day, a walk in the redwoods. When our lives become somewhat more spontaneous and we often skip our nap, Mokie jumps onto our bed after lunch and waits for us to join her in a nap, looking baffled when we prepare for our walk without napping first.

In anticipation of her favorite after-dinner treat, she studies my every gesture for an hour, preparing for the moment when I sit on the couch. That's her cue to sit at my feet, silent and erect, not begging or whining but in full expectancy. When I hold out her favorite treat, a chicken-treat-wrapped rawhide, her eyes bulge and she snatches it for thirty minutes of bliss.

When she's particularly content, she purrs and rolls over onto her back, spread-eagled, sometimes curling her body to one side into a curious and hilarious C-shape. The various ways she wags her docked tail and swings the entire lower half of her torso speak volumes from buoyant pride to ecstatic rambunctiousness. When we encounter several trails converging, she looks at me with her head tilted as if to say, "Which way, boss?" As soon as I point or nod in the direction we will take, she bolts off, leading the way with authoritative devotion. Her devotion is unconditional.

By the time Mokie comes into our lives, George and I have learned enough about ourselves and dogs from Cobbie the Terrier Mix, Lady the Keeshond, and Gucci the Pit Bull Mix, to fully appreciate everything about this Springer Spaniel. From total know-nothings, we have become dog aficionados. We understand why people want to clone their pets. We are simply in love with ours.

SUE EZEKIEL

HAIKU STROKE

May-June, 2021

SO, IT BEGINS
I said "Dark Water"
instead of "English Breakfast."
I couldn't name Grace.

I called her "the girl
with the long red hair upstairs."
We called 9-1-1.

The paramedics,
warm and gentle, guessed my words.
I tried to make sense.

I stayed for three days
in the hospital, my heart
pounding, beat by beat...

WHOOSH! Wild-fresh-crisp air,
flying free to my wheelchair
on Tanya's blues eyes.

I don't *need* to ride
my wheelchair. All that is wrong
is my mixed-up talk.

Who am I, when I
can't write and read? Anything?
Yes...my soul whispers.

Thirteen years of health
with such long, grim suffering.
And yet, such love-joy-life.

MY FIRST STROKE HAIKUS
Willy wonky words
Bumble bees wisteria.
Sweet nectars, joyful.

Golden wobbly moon
holds gnarly eucalyptus.
Deep rich roots ground life.

SPEECH THERAPY
"I'm reading great now!"
"You're up to third-grade level."
Ouch. Much more practice.

So much exhaustion.
I nap morning, afternoon,
and still sleep all night.

But in between, such
heaven: birds, penetrating
sun-warm, flowers, spring.

My *New Yorker*: What
to do with that subscription?
I can't read it well.

Will my therapist
think I should try to read it?
She might understand.

But Miriam says
I should read Talk of the Town,
the fun short stories.

ALPHABET WORDS
I worked on word games
for speech therapy: five fruits
per letter. Try "X!!!"

"My brain is worn out
from doing the five-fruit words."
Miriam gaffaws.

"It's only *one* word!
And it includes veggies, too!"
Eggplant saved the day.

Apples, berries, **C**
for lush Cara-Cara yum.
Dates, helped with a clue.

The clued **Eggplant. Figs.**
Grapefruit. What's **H? Jicama.**
(Does **Iced Mango** count?)

Kale. Limes. Mangos. Nuts.
Oranges. Pineapple. What's **Q?**
Raisins. Satsumas.

Turnips. Uva, yes?
Watermelon. Yellow squash.
X and **Z** elude.

My brain is muddled.
I need to rest, even nap.
Maybe more words then!

DAILY LIFE
When my mind settles
My thoughts enliven, awake.
Again, words begin.

I can't do two things:
Speak while angry or drinking.
How's that for karma?

I'm a kerfuffle
when expressing upset thoughts.
My brain is unwired.

I can read some things,
not others: *The Atlantic,*
not *The New Yorker.*

It has to do with
all those parenthetical
sections that lose me.

The Atlantic rolls
along smoothly, easily,
and makes me feel smart.

Every day I nap,
leaning in fluffy pillows,
mind loose, floating, free.

MARTINA REAVES

WHO WE ARE

In 2010, after taking memoir-writing courses from Deborah Lichtman at Berkeley's Osher Lifelong Learning Institute (OLLI), a small group of writers continued to work together. We named ourselves the Addison Street Writers Circle (ASWC) after Addison Street in Berkeley, where we met in a community room. Three years later, the room became unavailable, and we decided to meet in members' homes. Since Covid struck in 2020, we have been meeting on Zoom.

For productive and comfortable sessions, we have capped our membership at ten women. We meet weekly on Thursday mornings for two hours, and each member takes a turn at facilitating. Originally the facilitator brought an excerpt from a writer. We discussed this work, and we usually wrote from the facilitator's suggested prompts. But we have evolved. The facilitator now brings her own writing, and we spend the first 45 minutes evaluating her piece, giving positive feedback and suggesting improvements. Then we write, and we end the meeting with free-flowing discussion.

Our process has led to four members completing their memoirs; three have been published. These are Anna Rabkin's *From Kraków to Berkeley: Coming Out of Hiding*, Vallentine Mitchell, 2018; Martina Reaves' *I'm Still Here*, She Writes Press, 2020; Karen Grassle's *Bright Lights, Prairie Dust*, She Writes Press, 2021; Vivian Pisano's memoir will be released in 2022 by IngramSpark.

SUE EZEKIEL, a retired psychotherapist, is a first generation American, born and raised in the Bronx, New York. She lives in the Oakland Hills with her husband of sixty-one years. When she's not engaged with her family, friends and communities or hiking the Oakland Regional Park trails, she's working on her latest writing project, revising forgotten drafts and collecting them to leave a trace of herself for her children and grandchildren. She helps ASWC stay organized by updating documents related to our weekly schedule, pre-Covid annual retreats (hopefully to be resumed post-Covid), and our annual *Berries from Brambles*.

KAREN GRASSLE will celebrate the publication of her memoir, *Bright Lights, Prairie Dust*, after years of encouragement from ASWC! Her book is being published this November 2021 by She Writes Press, an indie publisher in Berkeley. Best known for her iconic role of "Ma" on the still-running series "Little House on the Prairie," Karen continues to act (though curtailed by the pandemic) both locally and throughout the US. She enjoys life in the Bay Area, where her son is also living and working. A founder of ASWC, she also participates in a number of charitable organizations including The Actors Fund, which has done so much to help performers and others during the pandemic. www.KarenGrassle.net

RUTH A. HANHAM and her husband, a congenial fellow-historian from New Zealand, live danger-ously among the tinder-dry hills of Kensington. A faculty brat, she grew up in Berkeley, traitorously decamped to Stanford, and thence to Harvard for a Ph.D. in history. She won a guest editorship on *Mademoiselle* magazine. She taught in Hong Kong, India, and at a small university near Boston. She branched out into the field of old age care and policy, served as vice-president of the Massachu-setts Committee for Elder Affairs, and went as a state delegate to the White House Conference on Aging. She re-settled in England when her husband became head of a university there, and she con-tinued writing. Finally, back to the Bay Area, where literary endeavors continued. Over the years she has had a modest number of articles published in professional journals, a women's magazine, and the *Journal of Public Health.*

ELEANOR LEW was born in Chinatown, San Francisco. She has lived and worked in Austria, Eng-land, Taiwan, Tunisia, India and Washington, D.C. Over the years she accumulated four academic degrees: in biology and genetics, Chinese literature and anthropology, international relations, and psychology. She has, at last, come home to herself as a marriage and family therapist. Eleanor has had three of her essays published by *The New York Times*: "One Moment You See, Then You Don't," "Travelers in the Dark," and "Doctor, I'm Going Blind. Why Won't You Talk to Me?" Eleanor con-tinues to write while working with her clients and facilitating a low-vision support group.

VIVIAN PISANO was born in Chile to a Chilean father and an American mother. At the age of ten, she came to the U.S. with her mother, sister and brother to live in Sacramento, California. In the mid-1970s she moved to the San Francisco Bay Area to pursue a master's degree in librarian-ship. She ultimately found her home in Berkeley, where she lives with her husband. Vivian has been writing personal essays, memoir, and short fiction since 2010, when she retired from a long career in librarianship. Her work has won awards and recognition, and several of her memoir/personal essay pieces have been published. She recently completed her memoir, *Living in Two Worlds: A Mem-oir*, which she will self-publish. Vivian enjoys the theater and even dabbles in acting, having taken classes at Stagebridge for several years. She enjoys the community of people she's met there, playing scenes together and meeting on Zoom for weekly play readings, and looks forward to attending live theater once Covid restrictions lift and theaters open their doors. www.vivianmpisano.com

KATE "CRICKET" POPE, a philosophy faculty brat, grew up in Berkeley. Despite two years at Stanford, she graduated from Cal. After wandering Europe for her post-graduation summer, she married in Paris, lived for six years in Germany, and returned to the Bay Area with three ener-getic offspring, soon joined by two more. She punctuated domesticity with backpacking, mountain climbing, ski racing, divorce at age 40, a master's degree, and gainful employment throughout. Her second marriage inaugurated three and a half decades of world travel characterized by a proclivity for high mountains and the untouristed locale. Kate, who at times appears to be using up her allot-ment of nine lives, writes stories from her life about close calls, memorable individuals, mountain adventures, travel mishaps, ski victories, and more.

ANNA RABKIN was born in Poland and spent her teenage years in England, France and, eventually, New York. She and her husband, Marty, migrated to Berkeley, where they raised their two children. Anna received a master's degree in City Planning, served as Berkeley's elected City Auditor for fifteen years, and upon retirement chaired the Berkeley Public Library Foundation's capital campaign for the Downtown Library while completing a graduate program in history. In 2003, she and four others founded the Free Agents at Berkeley (FAB), a network of retired women that has grown from 28 to 300 members. With her husband, she co-authored *Public Libraries: Travel Treasures of the West*, which was published in 1994 by North American Press.

In 2018, her memoir, *From Kraków to Berkeley: Coming out of Hiding*, was published in England by Vallentine Mitchell, the original publishers of Anne Frank's Diary. She has given many book talks focused on the issue of displacement both in the Bay Area, London, New York, and Montgomery, Ala. She was one of five authors featured at the YWCA's Festival of Women Authors and at the Berkeley Public Library Foundation Authors' Dinner. Articles about her book have appeared in *Berkeleyside, Hidden Child Magazine, J – Jewish News of No. California*, and the California State University, *East Bay's History Newsletter*. Excerpts from her book were included in the Heyday Press' 2019 book, *The Battle for People's Park, Berkeley 1969*, by Tom Dalzell. Just prior to Covid-19, she participated in the Julia Morgan School for Girls' Women of Courage Panel honoring Rosa Parks.

MARTINA REAVES grew up in a Navy family and lived in thirty-four places before she finally settled in her current home in Berkeley with her wife, Tanya, and their son, Cooper. She considers living in one place for thirty-five years a major accomplishment. A lawyer, she limited her practice to mediation in 1986 and worked with divorcing couples and neighbors with disputes. In 2007, she began writing fiction and memoir and has been at it ever since. Her memoir, *I'm Still Here*, was published by She Writes Press in April 2020. The book was awarded a Gold Medal from Living Now Awards (Grief/Death and Dying), a Silver Medal from Readers' Favorites (Non-fiction: Health/Medical), an IPPY Bronze award (Personal Struggle/Health Issues), a finalist in Best Book Awards (Health: Cancer), and a finalist in Best Books Awards (Health: Death & Dying). Her second memoir, *Ebb & Flow*, awaits final touches. In May 2021, Martina had a stroke that affected her writing and reading abilities. Her excellent speech therapists have done wonders, her skills increase weekly, and she is able to write and read again. www.martinareaves.com

MARYLY SNOW, Oakland born and the eldest of three girls raised by her divorced mother, retired from UC Berkeley's Architecture Visual Resources Library where she once received the honorific "Distinguished" in lieu of a 5% merit-based pay increase. She is proud of her payroll title of Distinguished Emerita Librarian. Maryly continues to be an active visual artist, printmaker (admitted by jury review to California Society of Printmakers in 1990), Zentangle teacher (Certified 2015), founder of the International Toothbrush Collection, beekeeper, bridge player, and book club reader. Always making art in a succession of Bay Area artist live-work lofts, she was active nationally helping develop access to images on the internet. Ten years ago she moved to a many-times-published small house at the end of the road in Chabot Canyon where she lives with her two cats, three beehives, and annual visits by herds of goats gobbling up wild mustard, star thistle, and fennel. In lieu of travel in the early Covid days, Maryly posted her first video to YouTube, featuring her *Pandemic Paradox* drawings (several of which were shown in *Berries From Brambles #11*). She exhibited her *Pandemic Paradox* drawings in 2021 in both Gwangju and Seoul, South Korea, and her installation piece with audio, *Tangled Climate Measurement Time,* in a series of *Extraction: Art at the Abyss* exhibits initiated by the Codex Foundation. www.snowstudios.com

LINDA NORTHRUP SONDHEIMER grew up and got her bachelor's degree in Buffalo, New York. In hippie girl adventure, she came to San Francisco in the 70s. It was love at first sight. Eventually, like many others, she realized that her painting degree was not an easy path to artistic credibility and financial remuneration. She found her true calling after graduate school and became an educator, truly the most creative thing she ever did. She is now retired, drawing, and writing fiction and memoir. This past November, her husband Fred traveled to whatever realm comes after this one. It was a weekend of family, poignant tears, appreciations, and love. She is now recovering from several surgeries, missing Fred, and planning her next chapter.

ADDISON STREET WRITERS CIRCLE
NOVEMBER 2021

Row 1: Martina Reaves — Maryly Snow
Row 2: Ruth A. Hanham — Linda Sondheimer
Row 3: Vivian Pisano — Eleanor Lew
Row 4: Kate Pope — Karen Grassle
Row 5: Sue Ezekiel — Anna Rabkin

OUR WEEKLY SHARED WRITINGS

Sue Ezekiel: "Something for Myself," "2020 Year of Disbelief and Outrage," "Dogs In My Life," "Recovering Hero Worshipper," "The Emphysema—Perestroika Migration."

Karen Grassle: "A Mammogram in the Pandemic."

Eleanor Lew: "One Person Can Make a Difference," "The Departed," "Excerpts on Hate," "Reasons for Hate," "Flamenco Dancers in Chinatown."

Ruth A. Hanham: "Miseries and Mysteries," "Gardener: Part One."

Vivian M. Pisano: "Best Friends," "Regrets," "On Getting the Vaccine," "Too Many Encounters," "Thirteen."

Kate Pope: "Traveling the World: The Course of True Love," "Evolution Valley Fiasco," "Entanglement of Names," "Lightning in the Bugaboos, Part One."

Anna Rabkin: "Marty and His Father," "Marty and His Father: Part II," "More to Life than Work," "A Gift from the Past," "Family Disruption."

Martina Reaves: "Moving."

Maryly Snow: "A COVID Christmas," "Bobo Lanky," "Finagling A Fence."

Linda Sondheimer: "The Last Honeymoon," "A Scar is a Story You Love to Tell," "Preface," "The Increments Are Small at First," "Magic Marc," "Words Fail," "Is It Time?"

www.ingramcontent.com/pod-product-compliance
Lightning Source LLC
Chambersburg PA
CBHW081104300726
48976CB00011B/2720

9 798985 013009